SKY HIGH
HAMPSHIRE COAST

PHOTOGRAPHY BY JASON HAWKES

First published in Great Britain in 2009

Photographs © 2009 Jason Hawkes

British Library Cataloguing-in-Publication Data
A CIP record for this title is available from the British Library

ISBN 978 1 906887 53 7

PiXZ Books
Halsgrove House, Ryelands Industrial Estate,
Bagley Road, Wellington, Somerset TA21 9PZ
Tel: 01823 653777
Fax: 01823 216796
email: sales@halsgrove.com

An imprint of Halstar Ltd, part of the Halsgrove group of companies
Information on all Halsgrove titles is available at: www.halsgrove.com

Printed and bound by Grafiche Flaminia, Italy

Introduction

Hampshire's coast runs from Highcliffe on the Dorset border to Chichester Harbour in West Sussex, a distance of about 55 kilometres (34 miles) as the crow flies. But the actual distance, following every creek and inlet of each harbour and estuary, is in excess of 370 kilometres (230 miles). This has produced a unique coastline, remarkably varied and important for many reasons, particularly for its commercial ports, wildlife, historic heritage, recreation, tourism and marine industries.

The area between the Hampshire coast and the Isle of Wight is known as The Solent. It is one of the busiest coastal zones in England, yet it retains areas of national importance for its landscape and nature conservation value. Hampshire's coast is highly valued by residents and visitors alike, and each will find the aerial photographs in this little book equally fascinating.

Sky High Hampshire Coast is the perfect keepsake.

Barton on Sea, looking down over Marine Drive.

Right: The view westwards over Barton on Sea, Highcliffe beyond and Christchurch far distant.

Looking west over Barton on Sea golf course towards Milford on Sea. The Isle of Wight can be seen on the far horizon.

Looking inland over Milford on Sea.

Left: Contemporary buildings and traditional beach huts at Milford on Sea.

Keyhaven, where the sandy spit of Hurst Beach encloses salt marsh, at the entrance to The Solent.

Keyhaven and Hurst Point, with the Isle of Wight beyond.

Left: Hurst Castle, one of a chain of fortifications built by Henry VIII along the south coast.

The marinas at Lymington.

The importance of leisure boating to Lymington is exemplified in this photograph.

The oil refinery at Fawley.

Left: On the west bank of the Lymington River, Lymington has a population of around 14 000.

Looking over WestQuay shopping centre, Southampton.

Right: The view north-east over Southampton.

Imported vehicles line the dockside, Southampton.

Left: The Isle of Wight ferry enters Town Quay, Southampton.

Southampton's Ocean Village Marina.

Right: The New Forest inland, with Eling Creek, Totton, on the right.

Hamble is world famous for its boatbuilding.

Millions of pounds literally 'tied-up' on the River Hamble

Burlesdon on the River Hamble.

Right: Exclusive riverside properties at Burlesdon.

Looking across the River Hamble towards Burlesdon.

Left: Low sun over the River Hamble, Hamble-le-Rice foreground, with Fawley across The Solent.

Warsash, at the mouth of the River Hamble.

Left: A bend in the River Hamble at Burlesdon, Sarisbury and Locks Heath distant.

A superb panorama of the coastline with Warsash in the middle distance, Lee on Solent visible up the coast far right.

The nationally important wildlife preserve at Titchfield Haven.

Right: Hillhead looking north towards Stubbington.

Formerly HMS *Daedalus* airfield lying between Hillhead and Lee-on-Solent.

Right: Lee-on-Solent, with Gosport and Portsmouth glimpsed in the distance.

The view over Alverstoke and Gosport, Portsmouth beyond.

Left: Stokes Bay overlooking Alverstoke.

Gosport peninsula, with Fort Gilkicker, commands the westward entrance to Portsmouth harbour.

Above and right: Two views into Portsmouth Harbour.

Portchester Castle stands on the site of an earlier Roman fort.

Right: Portchester Sailing Cub, a bird's eye view.

Above and right: Lock gates at Port Solent Harbour
enclose a 'village' built for yachties.

Cloned craft at Port Solent.

Right: Looking north-east towards Wymering and Cosham.

The M275 follows the shoreline around North End towards Portsmouth.

Portsmouth harbour, the Isle of Wight beyond.

A Brittany Ferry entering
Portsmouth Harbour.

Above and right: Views over Portsmouth from Gunwharf Quays.

The Esplanade and the green at Southsea Common. A hovercraft is drawn up on the shore at the Hoverport, seen to the right of the funfair.

Southsea Castle, built in 1544.

Right: South Parade pier, Southsea, first opened in 1897.

Low tide at Eastney harbour.

Left: The growth of knowledge: allotments at the edge of the University of Portsmouth campus.

Langstone Harbour.

Left: Fort Cumberland was built between 1785 and 1810 to protect Langstone Harbour.

Eastern Road bridge at Great Salterns connecting to Havant bypass.